To my beloved wife, whose unwavering love and support are the inspiration behind all of my achievements. With your kindness, patience, and constant encouragement, you make each day brighter and more meaningful. May this book serve as a small reflection of the brightness and joy you bring into my life. Thank you for being my greatest source of inspiration and for sharing this journey with me. With all my love and gratitude, this book is for you.

Vanderlei Santos

Digital Corpore

2024

THIS BOOK BELONGS TO

____

Vanderlei Santos
Digital Corpore
2024

SPACE TO TEST YOUR COLOR

SPACE TO TEST YOUR COLOR

SPACE TO TEST YOUR COLOR

SPACE TO TEST YOUR COLOR

SPACE TO TEST YOUR COLOR

SPACE TO TEST YOUR COLOR

SPACE TO TEST YOUR COLOR

SPACE TO TEST YOUR COLOR

SPACE TO TEST YOUR COLOR

SPACE TO TEST YOUR COLOR

SPACE TO TEST YOUR COLOR

SPACE TO TEST YOUR COLOR

SPACE TO TEST YOUR COLOR

SPACE TO TEST YOUR COLOR

SPACE TO TEST YOUR COLOR

SPACE TO TEST YOUR COLOR

SPACE TO TEST YOUR COLOR

SPACE TO TEST YOUR COLOR

SPACE TO TEST YOUR COLOR

SPACE TO TEST YOUR COLOR

SPACE TO TEST YOUR COLOR

SPACE TO TEST YOUR COLOR

SPACE TO TEST YOUR COLOR

SPACE TO TEST YOUR COLOR

SPACE TO TEST YOUR COLOR

SPACE TO TEST YOUR COLOR

SPACE TO TEST YOUR COLOR

SPACE TO TEST YOUR COLOR

SPACE TO TEST YOUR COLOR

SPACE TO TEST YOUR COLOR

SPACE TO TEST YOUR COLOR

SPACE TO TEST YOUR COLOR

SPACE TO TEST YOUR COLOR

SPACE TO TEST YOUR COLOR

SPACE TO TEST YOUR COLOR

SPACE TO TEST YOUR COLOR

SPACE TO TEST YOUR COLOR

SPACE TO TEST YOUR COLOR

SPACE TO TEST YOUR COLOR

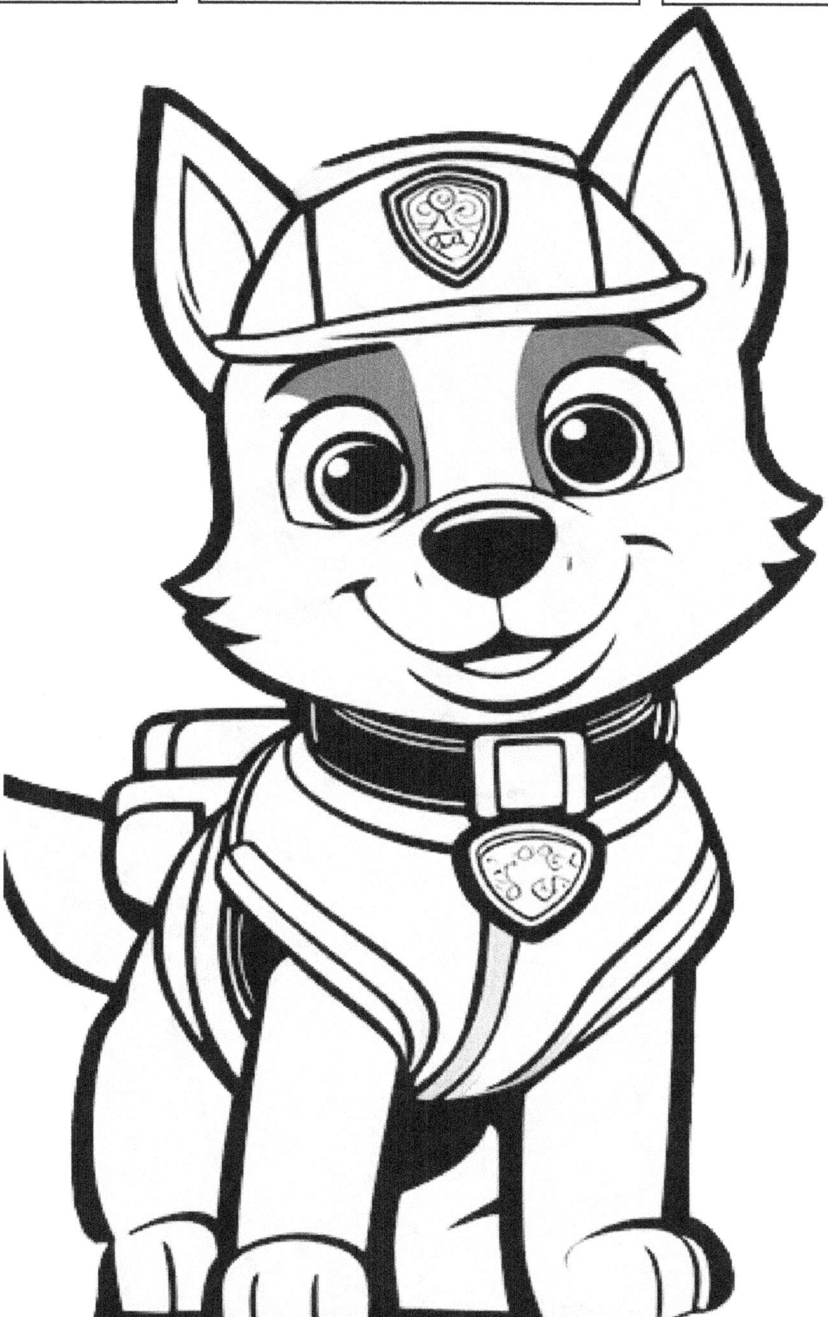

SPACE TO TEST YOUR COLOR

SPACE TO TEST YOUR COLOR

SPACE TO TEST YOUR COLOR

SPACE TO TEST YOUR COLOR

SPACE TO TEST YOUR COLOR

SPACE TO TEST YOUR COLOR

SPACE TO TEST YOUR COLOR

SPACE TO TEST YOUR COLOR

SPACE TO TEST YOUR COLOR

SPACE TO TEST YOUR COLOR

SPACE TO TEST YOUR COLOR

SPACE TO TEST YOUR COLOR

SPACE TO TEST YOUR COLOR

SPACE TO TEST YOUR COLOR

SPACE TO TEST YOUR COLOR

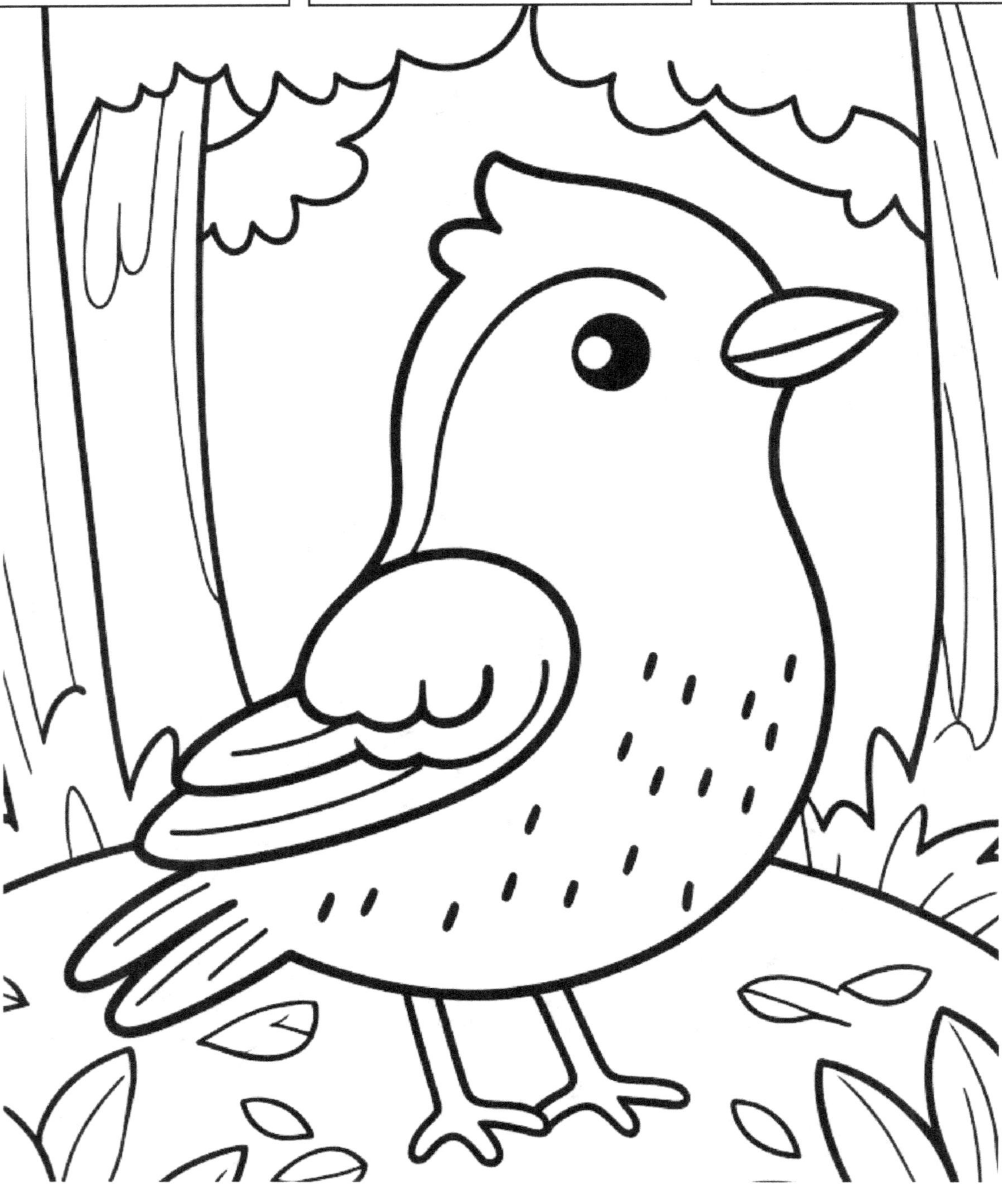

SPACE TO TEST YOUR COLOR

SPACE TO TEST YOUR COLOR

SPACE TO TEST YOUR COLOR

SPACE TO TEST YOUR COLOR

SPACE TO TEST YOUR COLOR

SPACE TO TEST YOUR COLOR

SPACE TO TEST YOUR COLOR

SPACE TO TEST YOUR COLOR

SPACE TO TEST YOUR COLOR

SPACE TO TEST YOUR COLOR

SPACE TO TEST YOUR COLOR

SPACE TO TEST YOUR COLOR

SPACE TO TEST YOUR COLOR

SPACE TO TEST YOUR COLOR

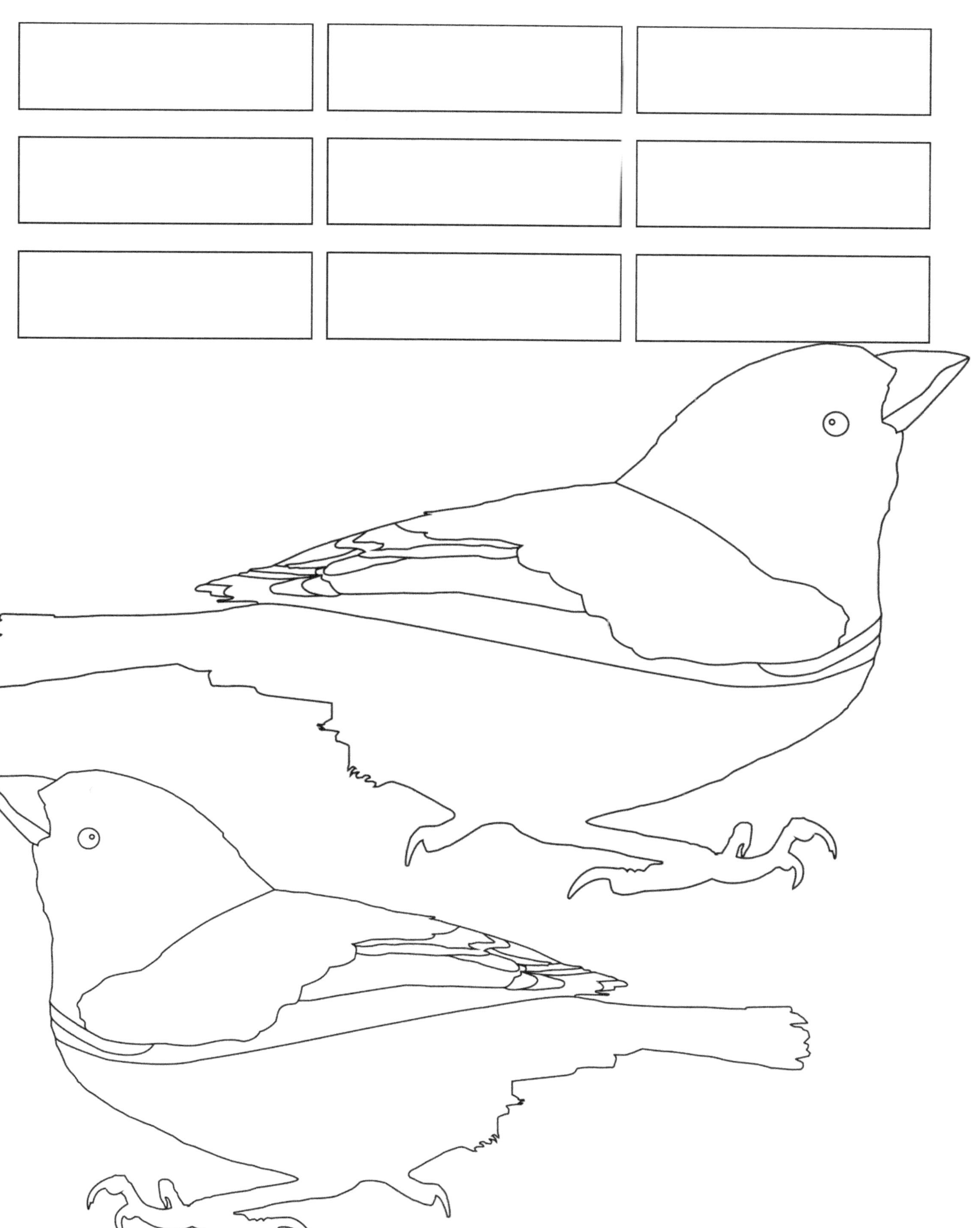

SPACE TO TEST YOUR COLOR

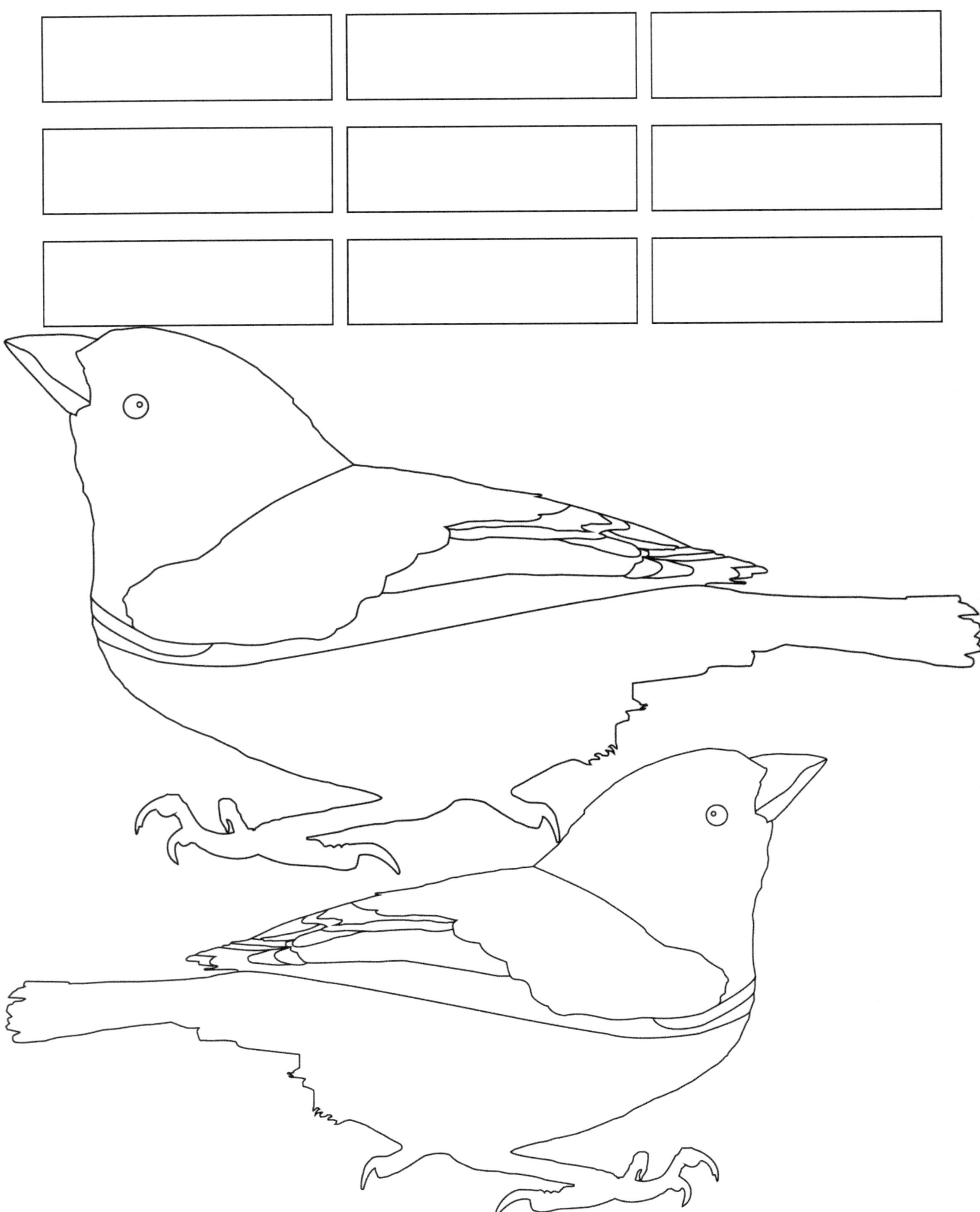

SPACE TO TEST YOUR COLOR

SPACE TO TEST YOUR COLOR

SPACE TO TEST YOUR COLOR

SPACE TO TEST YOUR COLOR

SPACE TO TEST YOUR COLOR

SPACE TO TEST YOUR COLOR

SPACE TO TEST YOUR COLOR

SPACE TO TEST YOUR COLOR

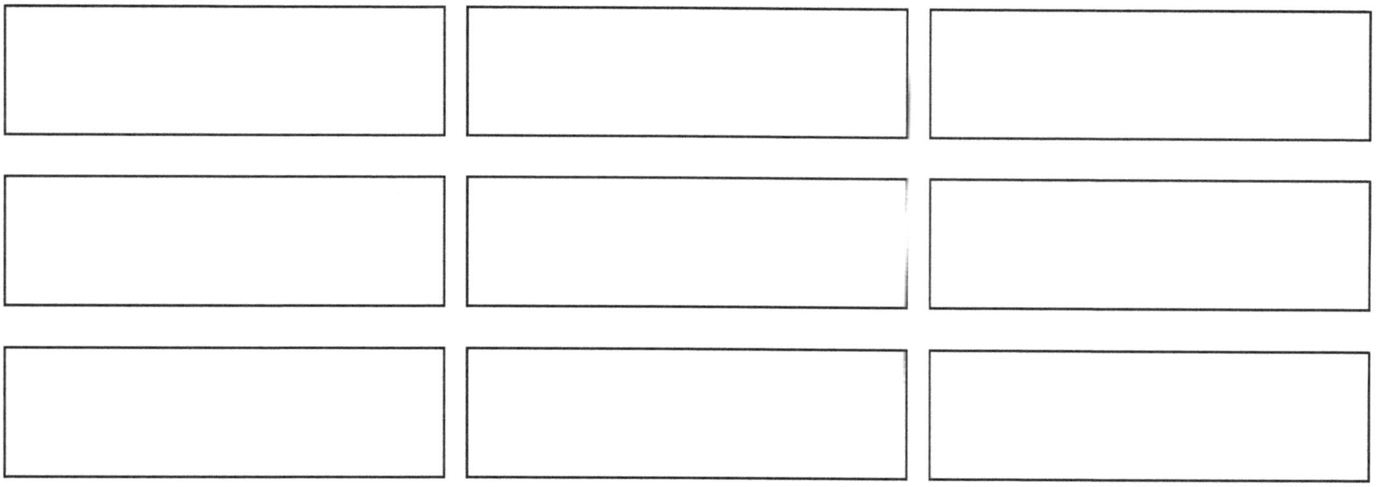

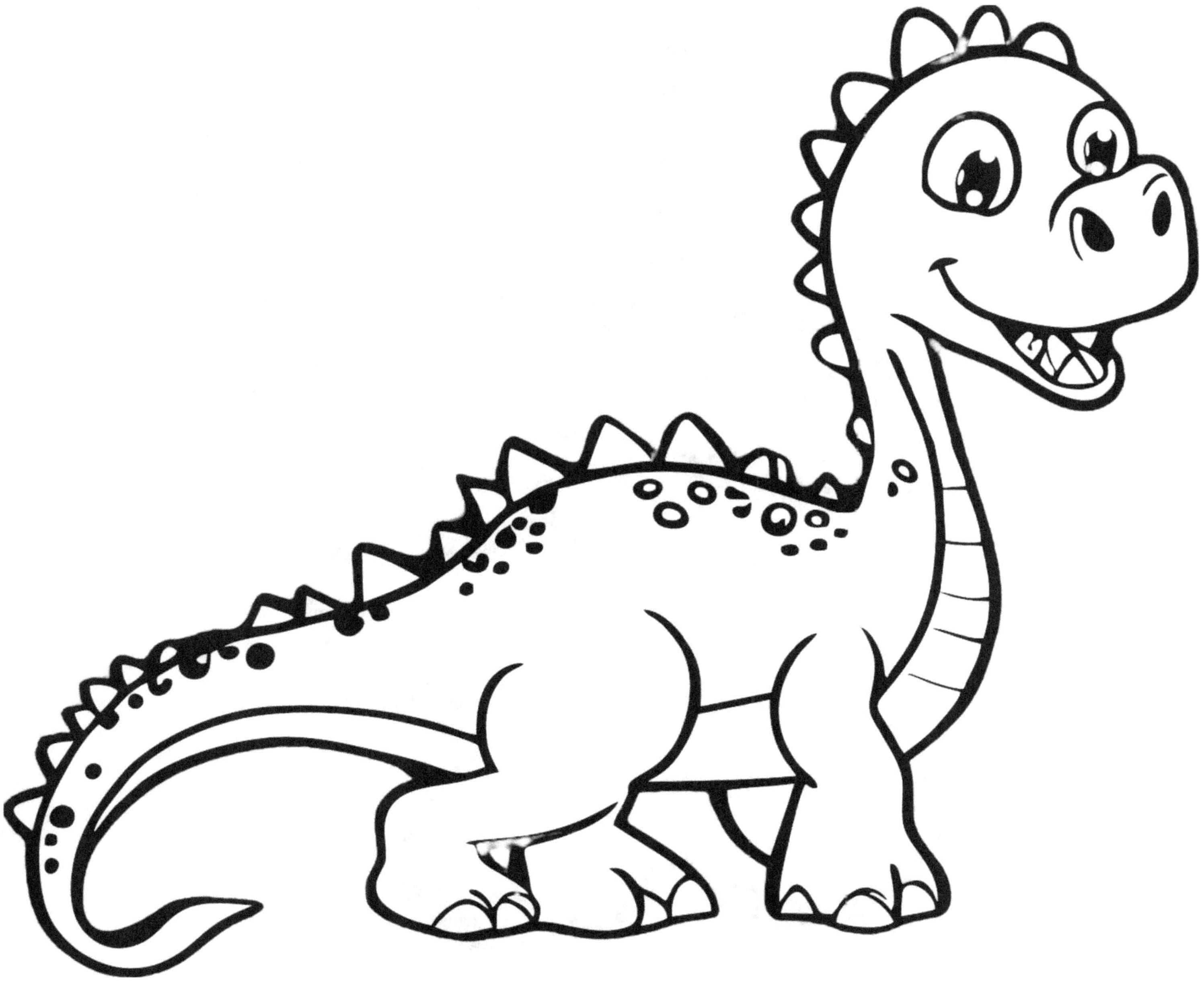

SPACE TO TEST YOUR COLOR

SPACE TO TEST YOUR COLOR

SPACE TO TEST YOUR COLOR

SPACE TO TEST YOUR COLOR

SPACE TO TEST YOUR COLOR

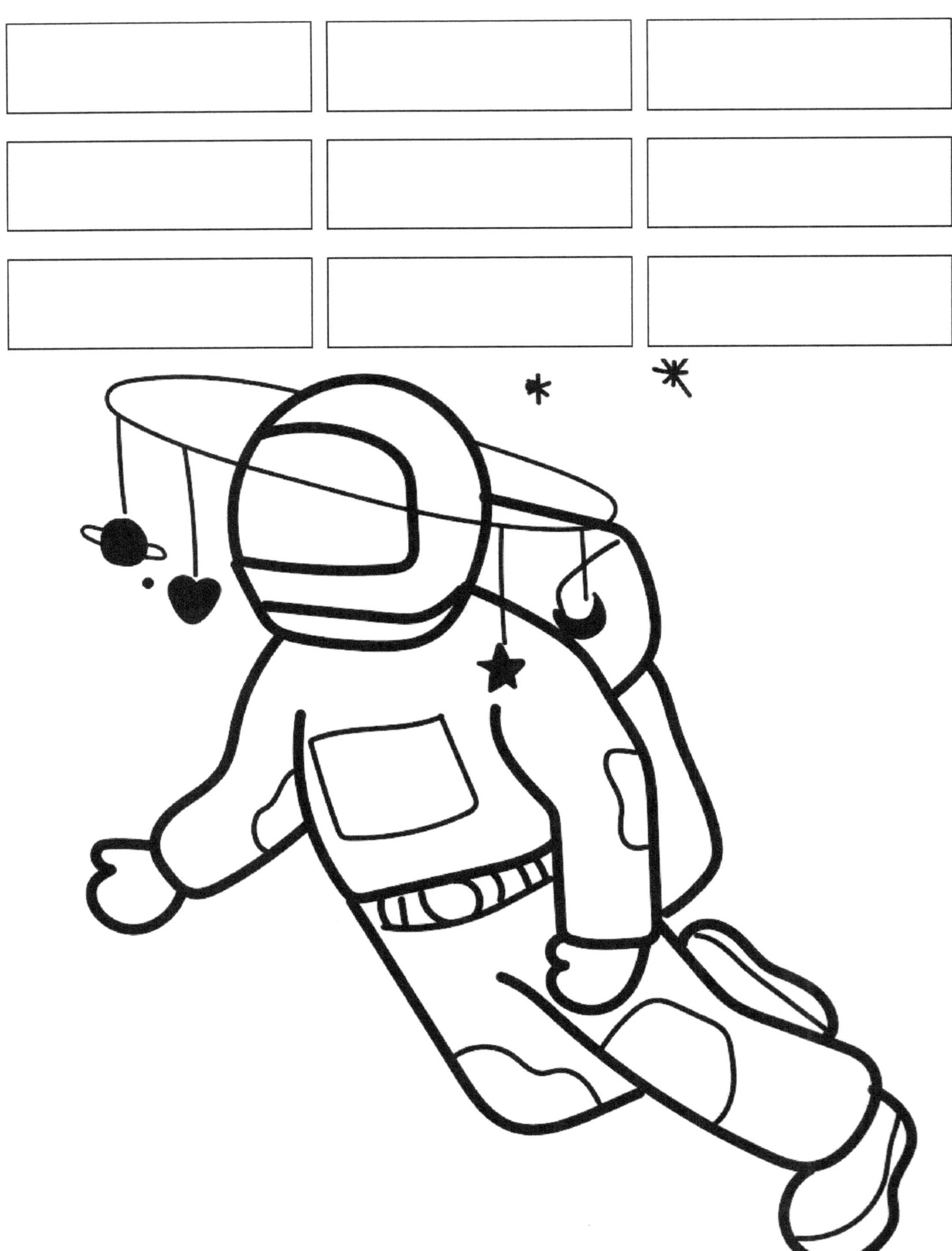

SPACE TO TEST YOUR COLOR

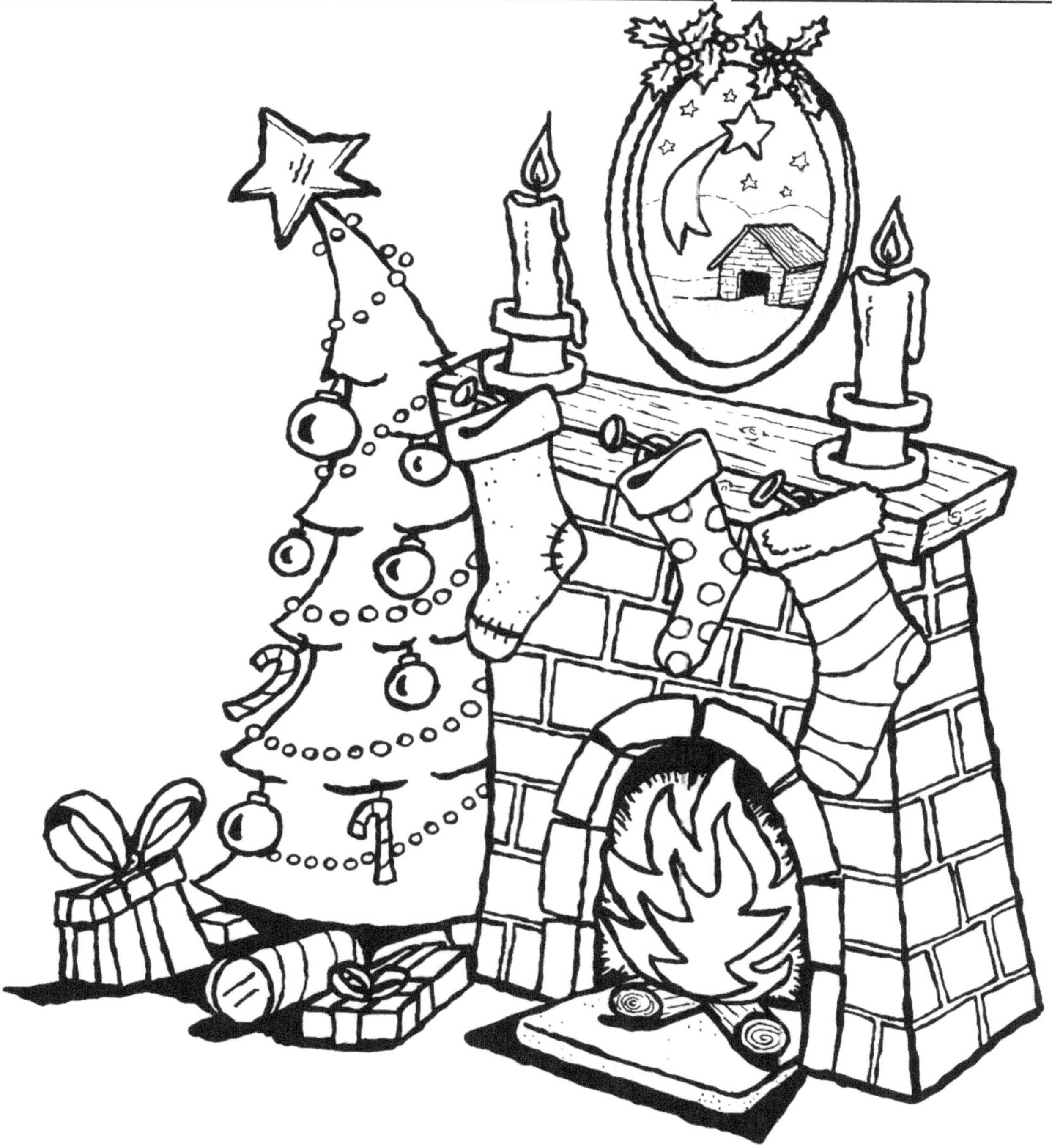

SPACE TO TEST YOUR COLOR

МОТНЕЯ

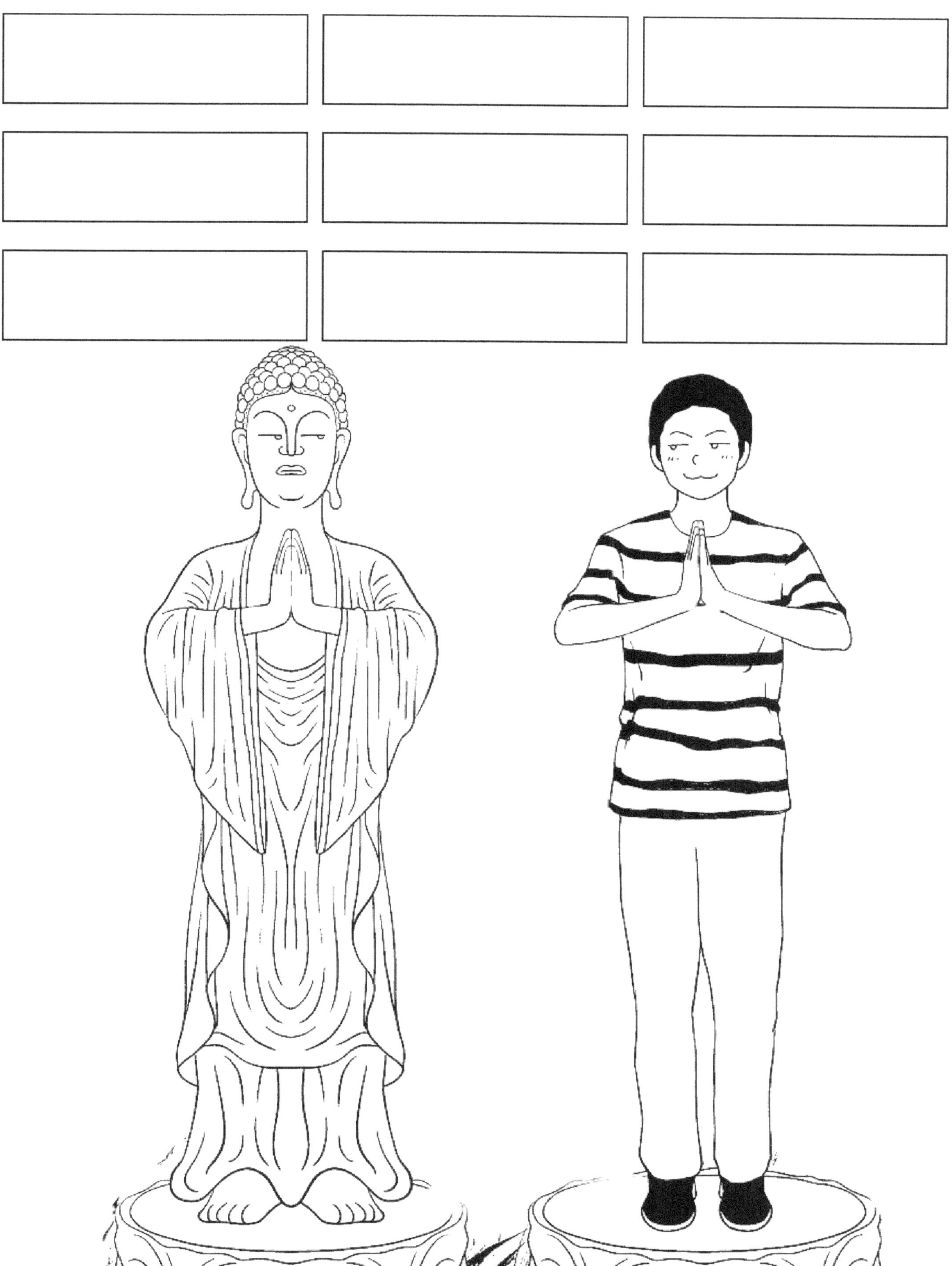

SPACE TO TEST YOUR COLOR

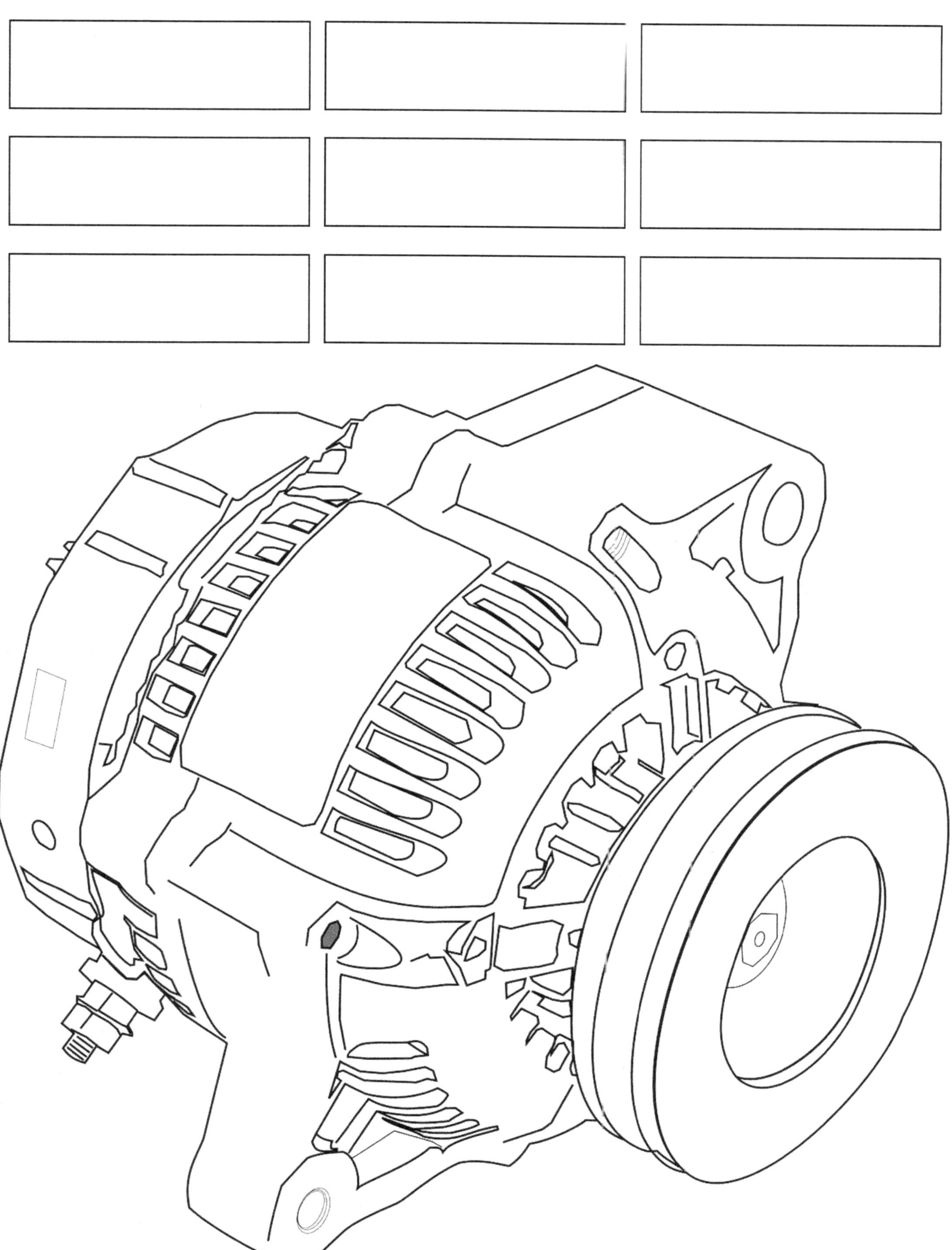

SPACE TO TEST YOUR COLOR

SPACE TO TEST YOUR COLOR

SPACE TO TEST YOUR COLOR

SPACE TO TEST YOUR COLOR

SPACE TO TEST YOUR COLOR

SPACE TO TEST YOUR COLOR

SPACE TO TEST YOUR COLOR

SPACE TO TEST YOUR COLOR

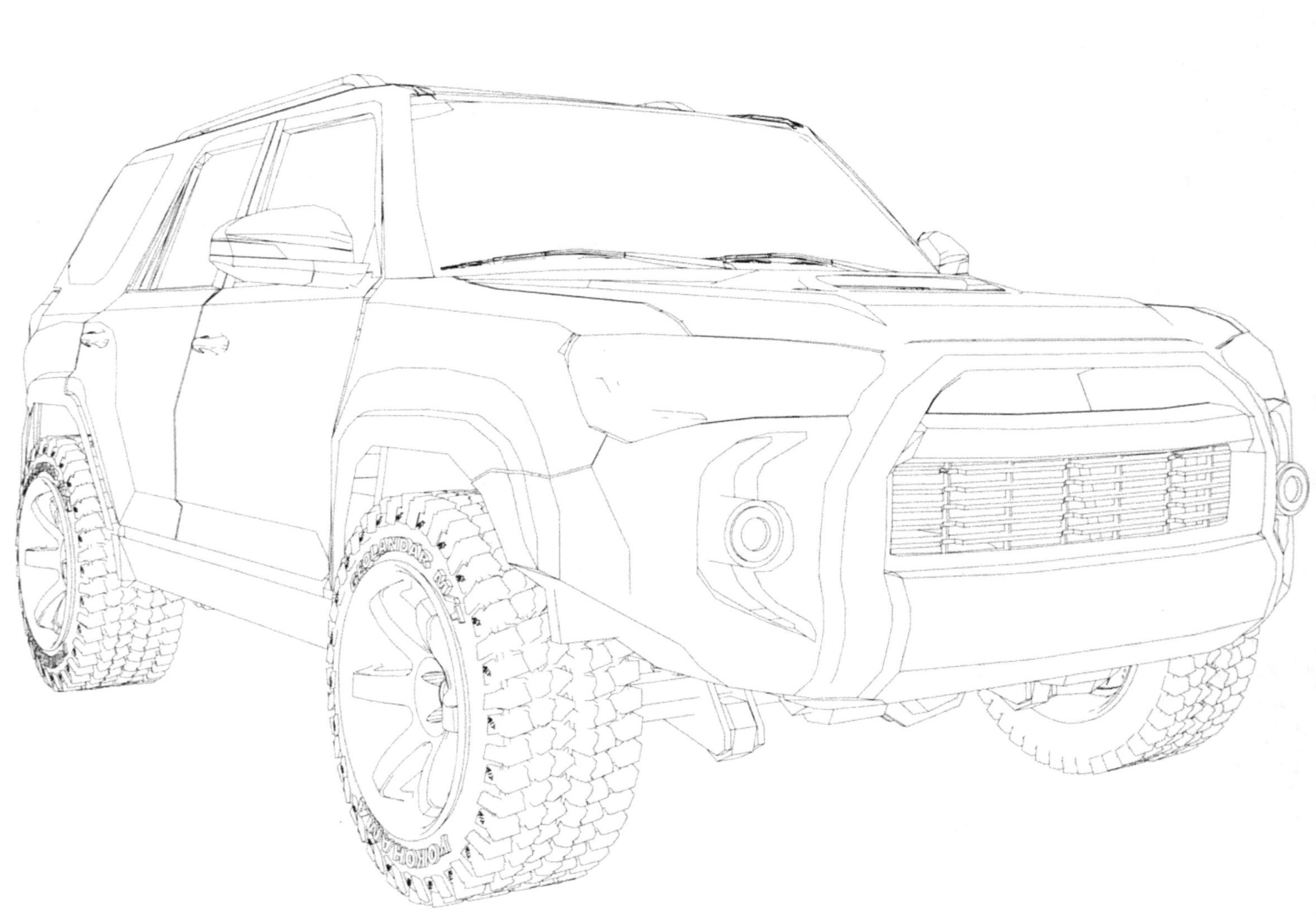

SPACE TO TEST YOUR COLOR

SPACE TO TEST YOUR COLOR

SPACE TO TEST YOUR COLOR

SPACE TO TEST YOUR COLOR

SPACE TO TEST YOUR COLOR

SPACE TO TEST YOUR COLOR

SPACE TO TEST YOUR COLOR

SPACE TO TEST YOUR COLOR

SPACE TO TEST YOUR COLOR

SPACE TO TEST YOUR COLOR

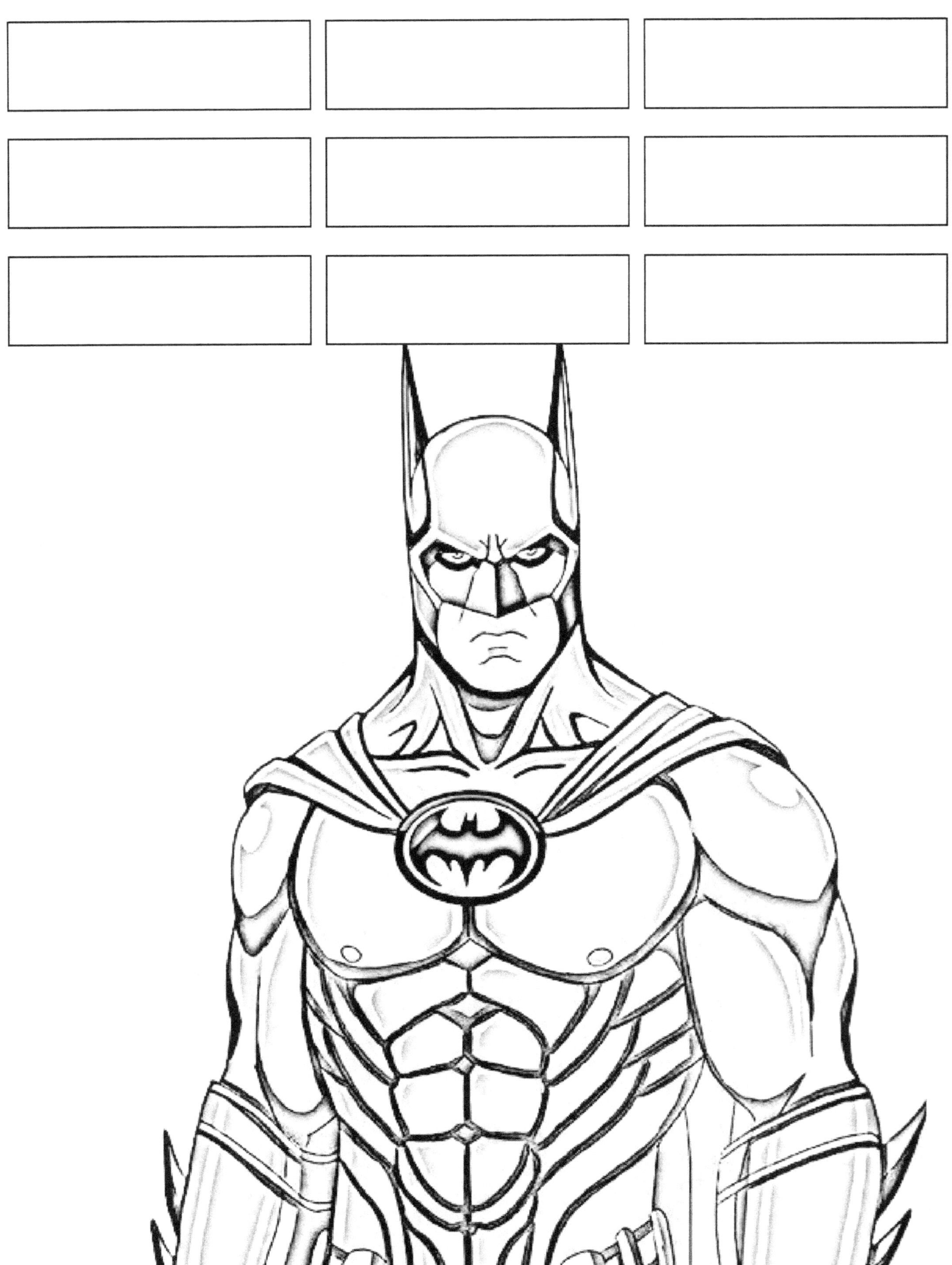

SPACE TO TEST YOUR COLOR

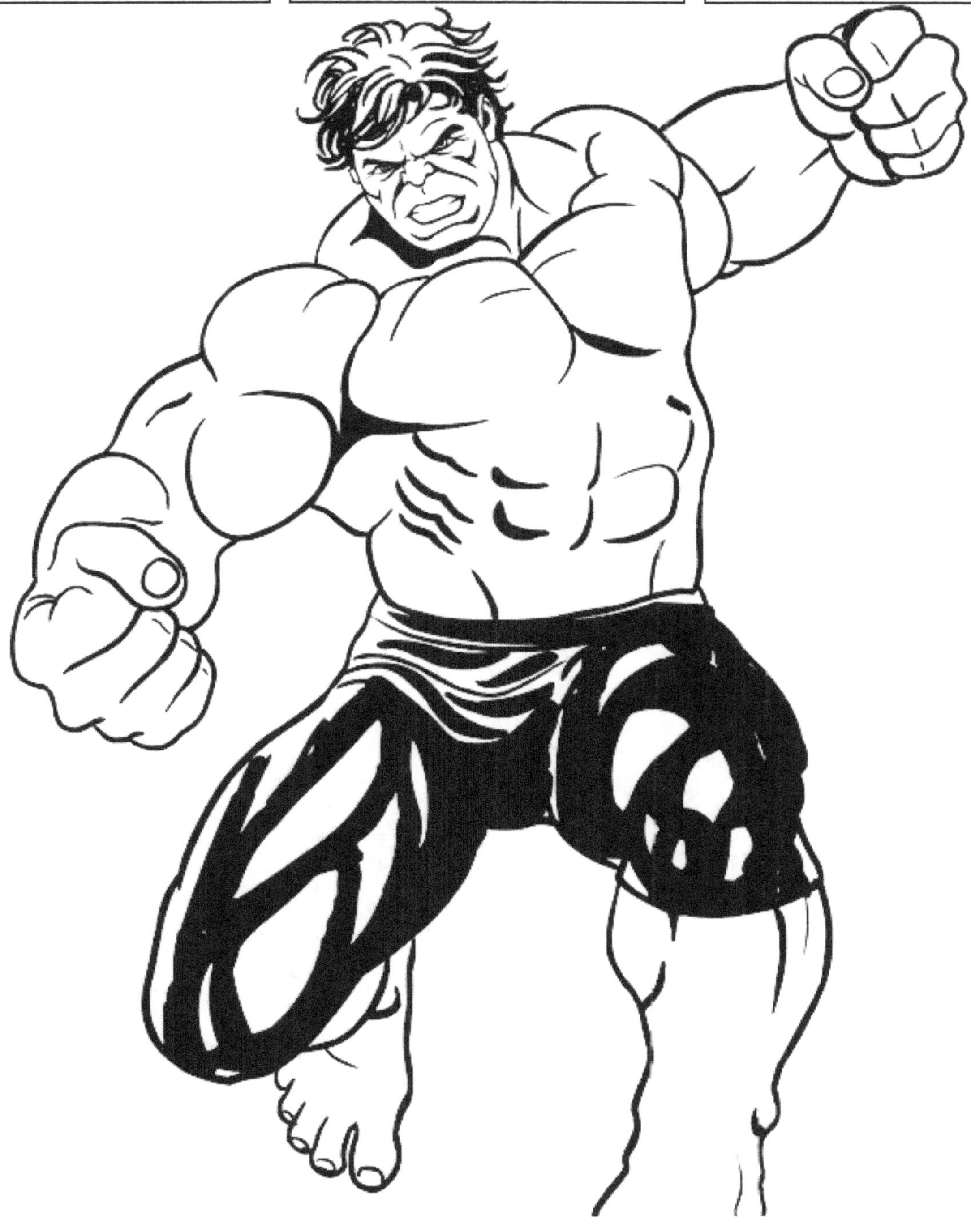

SPACE TO TEST YOUR COLOR

SPACE TO TEST YOUR COLOR

SPACE TO TEST YOUR COLOR

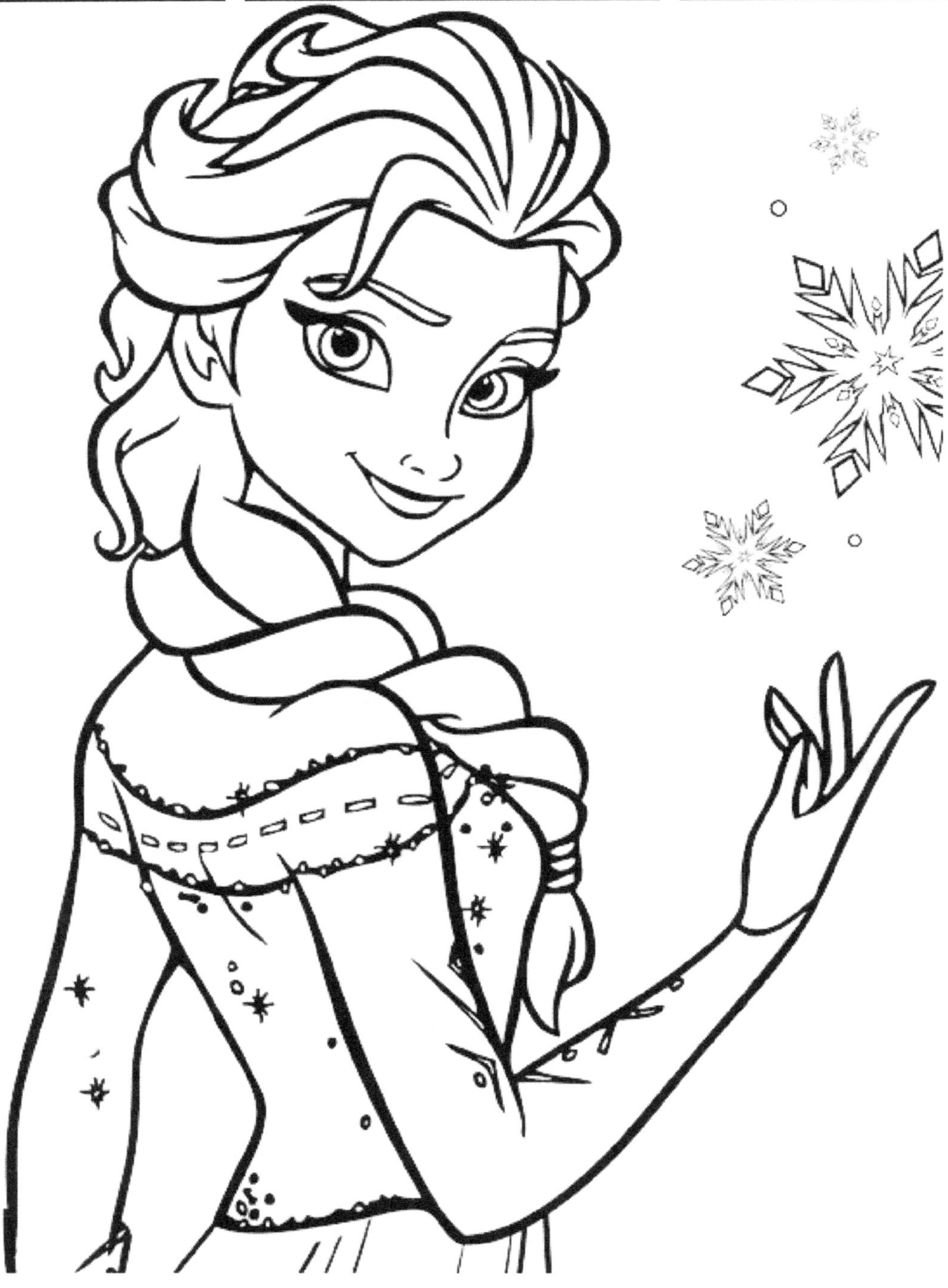

SPACE TO TEST YOUR COLOR

SPACE TO TEST YOUR COLOR

SPACE TO TEST YOUR COLOR

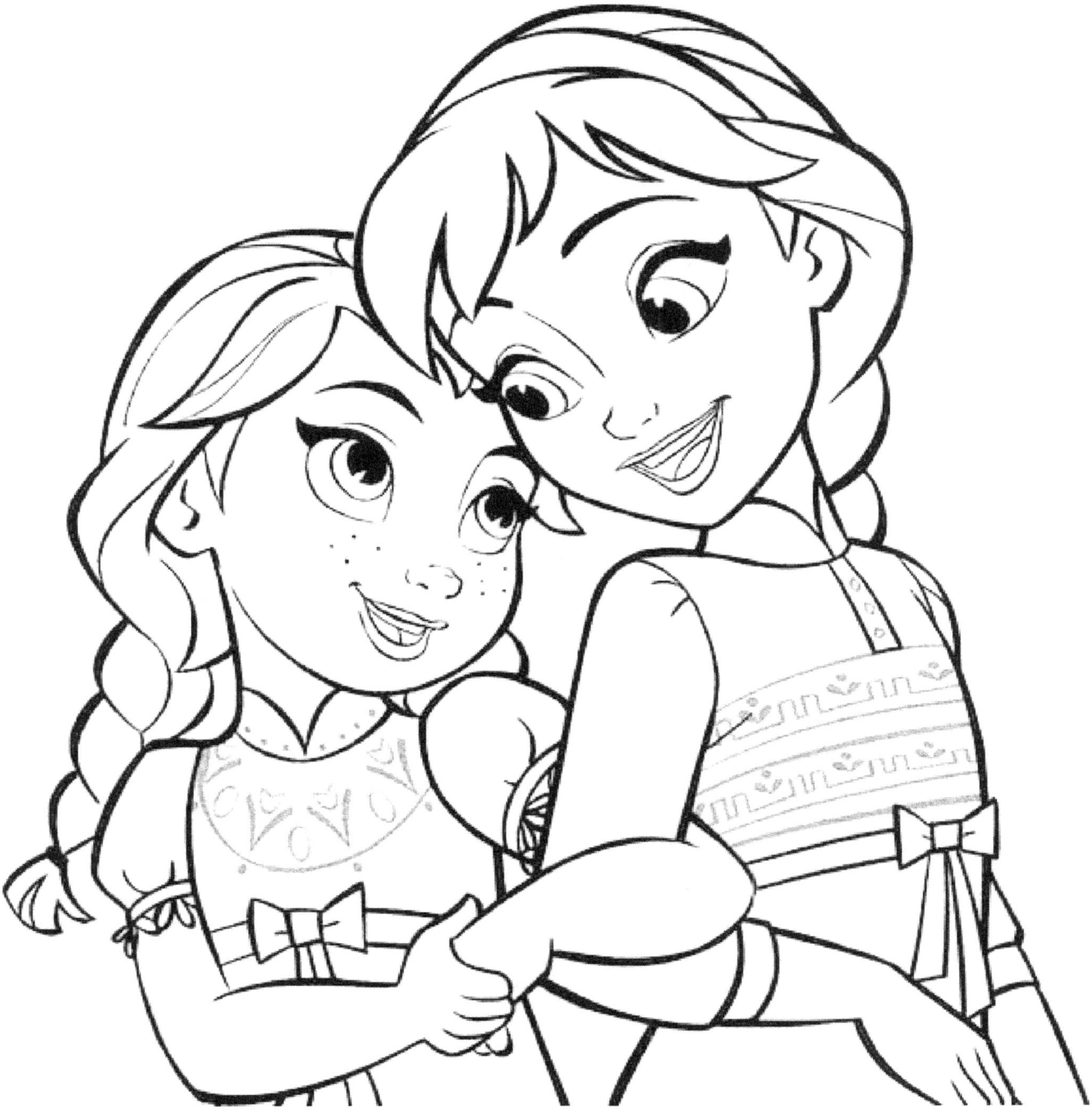

SPACE TO TEST YOUR COLOR

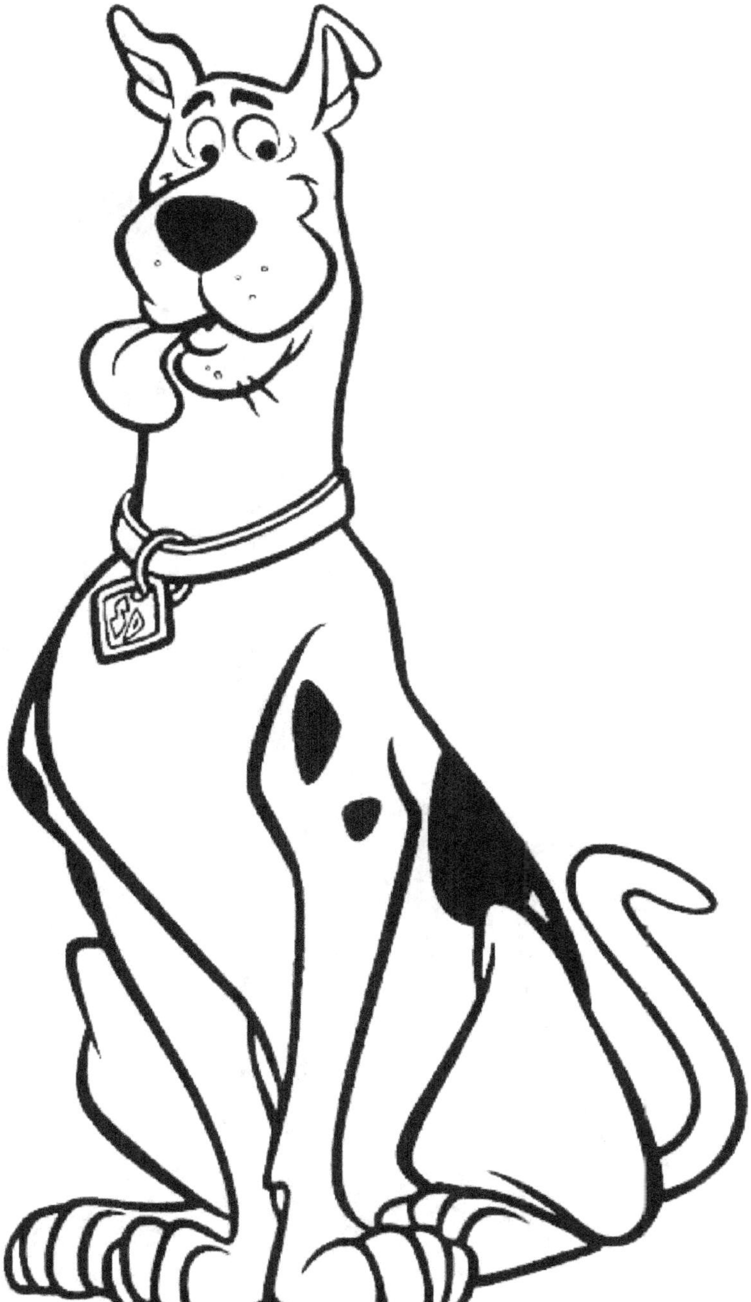

SPACE TO TEST YOUR COLOR

SPACE TO TEST YOUR COLOR

SPACE TO TEST YOUR COLOR

SPACE TO TEST YOUR COLOR

SPACE TO TEST YOUR COLOR

SPACE TO TEST YOUR COLOR

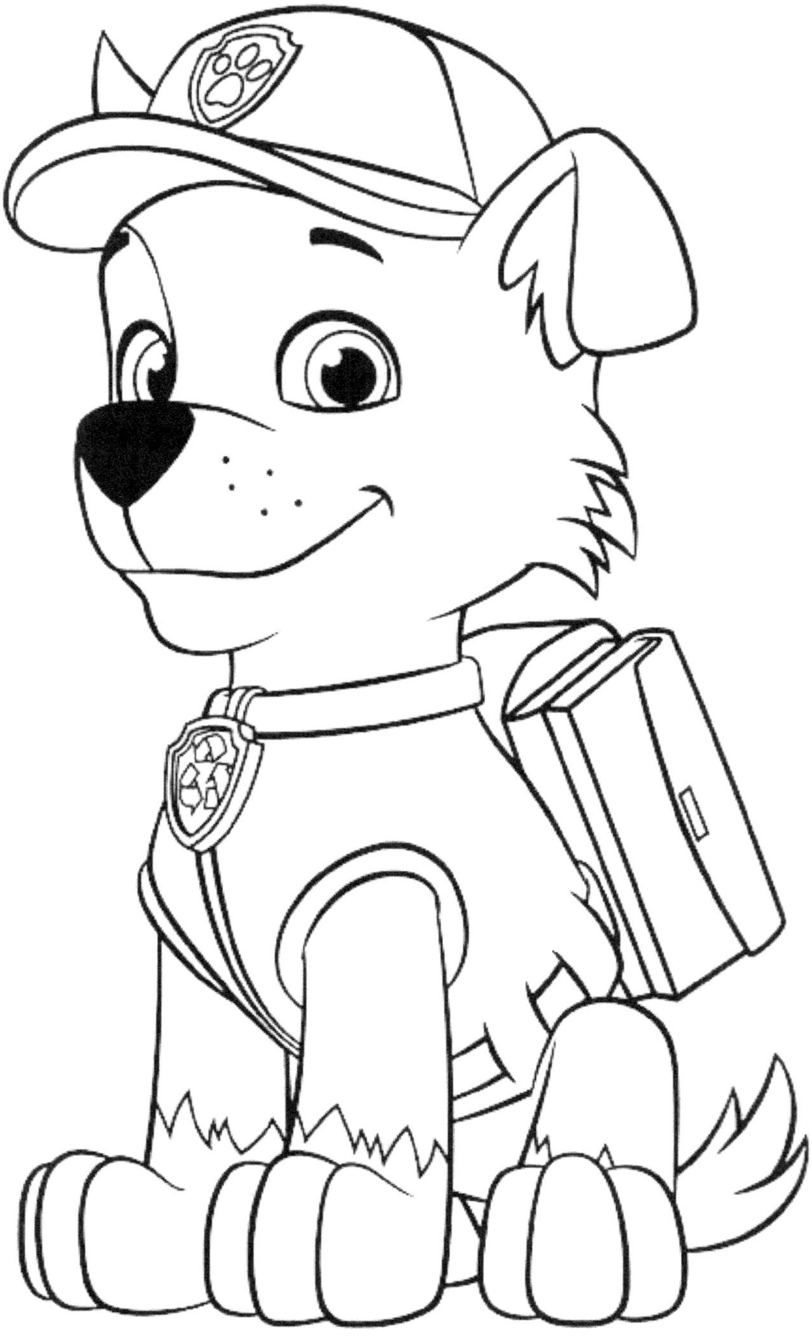

ZUMA

SKYE

SPACE TO TEST YOUR COLOR

EVEREST